Clean up!

Julia Lawson

Photographs by
Peter Millard

Evans Brothers Limited

We're
cleaning up today.
Let's start in the garden.
What tools do we need?

We are raking up the leaves.
What shall we use to put
them
into the
sack?

When there are lots of leaves, one machine blows them into big piles

and another sucks them up. Can you guess how they work?

Leaf Racing!
You can have lots of fun playing this game. Collect some leaves and arrange them in a line. The object of the game is to blow your leaf, using a straw if you want, as far as you can. How far did you blow your leaf?

Our boots are very muddy. We're hosing them down.

Our clothes are dirty too. We need to wash them. Do I need to sort them out first?

Oh dear! We'd better sweep up the mess.

Can you see how this road sweeper works?

We need to wash the floor now. What should we use?

Try doing some foot printing or use OLD shoes or wellington boots to make shoe prints. Afterwards try to guess which shoe made which print. Don't forget, you will have to wash the shoes and wellies. How will you do that?

**Throw it away!
Mop it up!
Wipe it dry!**

14

I can almost reach the ceiling ...

and I can reach into small corners.

Why does a vacuum cleaner make a noise? Mind my feet!

I wonder what these tools are for?

Clean Up Song
(to the tune of 'The Farmer's in the Dell')
Let's clean up today,
Let's clean up today,
Ee-I-Ah-Dee-Oh,
Let's clean up today.
We've had our fun,
Our day is done,
Ee-I-Ah-Dee-oh,
Let's clean up today.

Why not make up your own verses ... Let's dust today or Let's polish today?

We've cleaned up indoors and outside. It's all done ...

Oh no!

Try this action rhyme!
Wash the windows,
Wipe the door,
Sweep the carpet,
Scrub the floor.
Dust the table,
Come and see,
All's as clean, as
clean can be!

Notes and suggested activities for parents and teachers

We hope that you have enjoyed sharing this book and have tried out some of the additional ideas found in the activity boxes. Feel free to adapt them. For example, if children try the leaf racing on page 7, they could also arrange the leaves in a circle and blow them into a small hoop on the ground. When they have finished playing, they might want to make a leaf collage or do some leaf printing.

Here are some other activity ideas children could try, along with some suggestions for storybooks, websites and videos. They all tie in with the theme of cleaning up. Have fun!

Early science
Including children when you are cleaning up is a good way of introducing early scientific ideas. For example, children might enjoy experimenting with different methods of cleaning to find out the answers to the following questions:

- Is it better to use warm water or cold to clean paint pots?
- Does it make a difference if you use soap or not when you wash your hands?
- What happens when you put a paper towel on a wet patch?

Storybooks
Arthur, Clean Your Room! Marc Brown, Red Fox
The Scary Monster Clean Up Gang Anne Lewis, Honno
Squeaky Cleaners in a Muddle! Vivian French, Hodder
Street Cleaner M. Twinn, Child's Play
Cleaning Witch Cecilia Lenagh, Hippo
Henry and Horace Clean Up W. Menel, North-South Books

Action songs and games
Let's Clean Up!
(to the tune of 'Three Blind Mice')

Let's clean up, let's clean up.
Rake up the leaves, rake up the leaves.
Hose our boots and wash our clothes,
Hose our boots and wash our clothes,
Vacuum, polish, dust and sweep,
Let's clean up.
Let's clean up, let's clean up.
Wipe the tables, wipe the tables.
Wash the ceiling and scrub the floor,
Wash the ceiling and scrub the floor,
Vacuum, polish, dust and sweep,
Let's clean up.

The children will enjoy miming the
appropriate actions as they sing along.
Why not make up some extra verses?

The Cleaner's Coming!
Agree with the children a set of mime
actions to go with certain commands.
These could include: 'Clean the windows!'
'Sweep the floor!' 'Vacuum the carpet!'
'Dust the top of the cupboard!' 'Pick up
the rubbish!' The children have to mime the
correct action for each command.

Websites
www.bbc.co.uk/education/teletubbies/
playground

A number of games on this site may be
suitable and they change regularly.

Videos
Kipper *The Big Freeze and Other Stories*
(includes Big Owl's Bath), Hodder

Rosie and Jim *The Biggest Messes Ever*

Teletubbies *Here Come the Teletubbies*,
BBC

Teletubbies *'Uh, Oh!' Messes and Muddles*,
BBC

Index

Photography acknowledgements

page 6: With thanks to Black and Decker Ltd
page 11: Ecoscene
page 16: Courtesy of Dyson Ltd